Four Views on Women and Church Leadership

Should Bible-Believing (Evangelical) Churches Appoint Women
Preachers, Pastors, Elders, and Bishops?

Ron Highfield

Keledei
PUBLICATIONS

An Imprint of Sulis International
Los Angeles | London

FOUR VIEWS ON WOMEN AND CHURCH LEADERSHIP:
SHOULD BIBLE-BELIEVING (EVANGELICAL) CHURCHES
APPOINT WOMEN PREACHERS, PASTORS, ELDERS, AND
BISHOPS?

Keledei Publications
An Imprint of Sulis International
Los Angeles | London

www.sulisinternational.com

Library of Congress Control Number: 2017902994
Paperback ISBN: 978-1-946849-08-3
eBook ISBN: 978-1-946849-09-0

Also by Ron Highfield

Great is the Lord: Theology for the Praise of God. Eerdmans, 2008.

God, Freedom & Human Dignity: Embracing a God-Centered Identity in a Me-Centured Culture. Intervarsity Press, 2013.

The Faithful Creator: Affirming Creation and Providence in an Age of Anxiety. Intervarsity Press, 2015

The Thoughtful Christian Life: Essays On Living as a Christian in a Post-Christian Culture, 2014.

Christianity — Is It Really True? Responsible Faith in a Post-Christian Culture, 2015.

A Course in Christianity For an Unchurched Church, 2016.

Table of Contents

Introduction...1

On Behalf Of Secular Feminism (Taylor George)...............11

    Response To Taylor George (Hunter Johnson) 15

    Response To Taylor George (Mackenzie Prestige) 23

    Questions For Discussion 31

In Defense Of Evangelical Egalitarianism (Hunter
    Johnson) 35

    Response To Hunter Johnson (Taylor George) 41

    Response To Hunter Johnson (Mackenzie Prestige) 45

    Questions For Discussion 53

In Defense Of New Complementarianism (Mackenzie
    Prestige) 57

    Response To Mackenzie Prestige (Taylor George) 67

    Response To Mackenzie Prestige (Hunter
    Johnson) 71

    Questions For Discussion 79

On Behalf Of A More Excellent Way...................................85

    Questions For Discussion 99

Introduction

The church was born in conflict and nurtured in controversy, and it has rarely enjoyed a moment of respite since. Soon after Peter's sermon at Pentecost, believers began to ask whether gentile converts must keep the Law of Moses. Much of Paul's energy was consumed helping the church answer this question in the negative. Soon, some within John's churches began to ask whether Jesus was a real, flesh and blood human being or a phantom. In the succeeding centuries, the church had to clarify how Jesus and the Spirit were related to God the Father. Developments in the Thirteenth Century forced the church to grapple with the relationship between faith and reason. The sixteenth-century Protestant Reformation centered on the question of justification but also dealt with the number and nature of the sacraments and the authority of Scripture in relation to tradition. The rise of modern natural science compelled believers to ask how the Bible can be reconciled with the new scientific discoveries and theories.

The Contemporary Challenge

In our age, the church faces the challenge post-Christian, progressive culture poses to the Christian vision of human life. From the middle of the Seventeenth Century until quite recently, the dominant question posed was "Is Christianity true?" But over the last fifty years, the question has become "Is Christianity good?" Contemporary culture demands maximum liberty for individuals to pursue their private happiness, and it resents any restriction on that pursuit except the rule that we should not interfere with others' pursuit of their happiness.[1] From the dawn of the Enlightenment to today, this view of the self and human happiness has played an increasingly significant role in movements that urge liberation from all oppressive forces, governmental, social, and familial. And it animates the contemporary gender revolution, from the quest for women's equality in all dimensions of society to the transformation of binary, biological sex into a continuum of psychological gender identity. At stake in this struggle is the very idea that human beings are created by God, dependent on God, and responsible to God. Modern progressive culture represents nothing less than a New Declaration of Independence, this time not from the King of England but from the Creator of heaven and earth.

---

[1] I discuss the modern demand for unrestricted liberty in *God, Freedom & Human Dignity: Embracing a God-Centered Identity in a Me-Centered Culture* (Downers Grove: Intervarsity Press, 2013).

Why Write a Book on Women and Church Leadership?

Given the enormous challenge modern culture poses to Christianity's views of human nature, divine creation, and the human end, why am I writing a book on "women and church leadership"? The short answer is that I believe the two issues are connected in ways that make it impossible to address one without dealing with the other. The church is being forced by the surrounding culture to examine and clarify its thinking about the status of women in society, church, and family. Progressive culture demands that the church adopt the modern image of the self as autonomous and self-creative. It wants Christians to become signatories to its New Declaration of Independence. And the issues of women's equality and gender identity are the places where the decision will be made for this generation. So, the very essence and truth of Christianity comes under discussion here.

Unhappily, in my view, the church is not prepared for this struggle. Many Christians have so adapted to the spirit of the times that they have become unclear about the difference between the progressive vision of liberation and the Christian vision of human dignity and freedom. That women should be made equal to men in all spheres of society seems to them a self-evident truth. If progressive-leaning Christians think about it at all and feel the need for support from the Scriptures, they reinterpret the New Testament texts that restrict the role of women in view of such "weightier" principles as justification by faith, the "new creation," and oneness in Christ. On the other hand, many traditionalists simply reassert the "plain" meaning and absolute authority of those restrictive texts for the contemporary church. But few of disputing parties understand the full scope of the problem.

Why Another Book?

There are scores—if not hundreds—of books and articles on this subject already in print. Why another? Many of those works are massive, scholarly, and technical, and they give the impression of being written exclusively by theologians for theologians. They contain a bewildering array of subtle exegetical arguments that involve extensive studies of Hebrew and Greek words and complicated debates about the most accurate translations of Greek and Hebrew sentences. Their pages are punctuated with references to other scholarly works, which the author may have read but the reader has not. And the sheer number of biblical texts and themes addressed overwhelms the average reader. Many Christian readers, untrained in contemporary biblical studies and theology, feel as if they are witnessing the "clash of the Titans." They have no way of assessing who has the best argument. Indeed, after reading such works, many believers are more confused than before they opened them. They are tempted to choose the expert who confirms what they already believe on other grounds.

Four Views on Women and Church Leadership is a different kind of book with different aims. I wrote this book for the average believer who wants to think seriously about women and church leadership but does not have the time or inclination to read dozens of scholarly tomes. I don't refer to other works on the subject, and there are few footnotes. I do not labor over the meaning of Greek and Hebrew words or attempt to challenge or defend over-the-counter English translations of biblical sentences. The ideas and supporting evidence are placed on the page in front of the readers, and all they need to evaluate them is an English Bible and their own experience. The chapters are short, and so is the book. I don't offer this book as a substitute for the others. They have a place, and I have read many of them with profit. But in the end, I am convinced that this subject is much simpler than the thickness and difficulty of those books imply. After all the scholarly pens are still, and the theologians fall silent in exhaustion, ordinary believers will still need to make a decision with less than perfect knowledge and absolute certainty. I am convinced that this little book can help believers arrive at the point where they can make an informed decision about as well as they could by reading a room full of technical volumes.

Goals and Methods

This book does not offer simple solutions to these challenges. I hope to help church leaders and all engaged in this discussion to ask the right questions, get clear on the real issues, and take into account all the presuppositions and consequences of their decisions. For these reasons, I cast the book as a debate between three very different viewpoints: Secular Feminism, Evangelical Egalitarianism, and New Complementarianism. I chose these three perspectives because I believe together they set before us the central issues to be decided and the basic intellectual and practical options available. Each standpoint is presented by a fictitious character whose presentation will immediately be critiqued by the other two disputants. I believe the debate format will help readers think through this issue better than other approaches could.

Four Views on Women and Church Leadership uses fictional characters as disputants, and as far as I know no other book on this subject does this. Speaking not as myself but in the voices of imaginary disputants, each personifying a different philosophy, allows me to articulate each viewpoint clearly, firmly, and without inhibition. My imaginary characters don't have to worry about toeing a party line, offending their friends, being humiliated by their enemies, maintaining a scholarly reputation, or protecting their path to career advancement. Their feelings don't get hurt; they are not seeking disciples or angling for speaking engagements. I created these characters for one purpose, that is, to stimulate us to think about this important issue. None of them represents my thoughts exactly as I would express them, so I do not feel an obligation to defend them. I speak in my own voice only in this Introduction, in the Questions for Discussion found at the end of each of the four chapters, and in Chapter Four where I will challenge the basic premise of the whole contemporary debate and propose a new approach to the issue. I chose the first names of my speakers at random from a list of contemporary unisex names. They are neither male nor female. Nor do they speak on behalf of men or women. They are personifications of the viewpoints they articulate.

In Chapter One, Taylor George will speak for Secular Feminism. Hunter Johnson represents Evangelical Egalitarianism. Mackenzie Prestige will defend New Complementarianism. Although this book is written to Christians concerned about the roles of women in church life, I found it necessary to include a secular voice. Taylor George represents a powerful current in contemporary society. Secular Feminism exerts influence out of proportion and far beyond its relatively small inner circle. It draws on a deep intuition in the modern mind that thinks every person should be granted the maximum level of freedom consistent with the freedom of others. Secular Feminism projects a mood of self-confidence, and its assertive rhetoric puts contrary viewpoints on the defensive in the presence of a modern audience. No surprise here, for the wider culture views traditional outlooks on the role women as reactionary and morally suspect.

In Chapter Two, Hunter Johnson voices a position I am calling Evangelical Egalitarianism, sometimes called Biblical Egalitarianism. It attempts to argue, contrary to the opinions of secular feminists and traditionalists, that the Bible does not approve of patriarchy; it actually teaches equality. Evangelical egalitarians work for the equality of men and women in all dimensions of church life while preserving the truth of evangelical Christianity and the authority of the Scriptures. Hunter must defend the egalitarian position on two fronts, rebutting the charge by secular feminists and traditionalists that egalitarian values and biblical faith are incompatible. Secular feminists urge Hunter to give up evangelical Christianity in favor of equality, while the traditionalist Mackenzie Prestige presses Hunter to give up egalitarian ideals in favor of biblical authority. Through the voice of Hunter I try to make the best case for the compatibility of biblical Christianity with the egalitarian system. However, the counter arguments of Taylor George and Mackenzie Prestige demonstrate that this reconciliation will be far from easy.

In Chapter Three, Mackenzie Prestige defends a position I call New Complementarianism, a point of view I will allow Mackenzie to explain. In many discussions, positions like Mackenzie's are labeled by their opponents "hierarchical" or "patriarchal," rather unjustly I think. But negative stereotypes will not intimidate Mackenzie who will speak boldly and aggressively, saying what many think but dare not say for fear of being ostracized and persecuted. And even if readers find Mackenzie a bit blunt for their tastes, it is imperative to hear the full argument, because it does something I've never heard done before. It addresses, head-on and unapologetically, the charge that the New Testament's restrictions on women arise from irrational prejudice. It turns the tables on its critics and claims that New Complementarianism offers a higher, more just and loving view of women than Egalitarianism does. Egalitarian philosophy is harmful to women, urges Mackenzie, and promotes exploitation by men, but New Complementarianism inspires a loving and protective attitude in men that is good for women.

In Chapter Four, I challenge the presuppositions and conditions that make the contemporary debate about women in church leadership inevitable. Over the centuries, the church transformed itself from an extended family, whose sole purpose was to serve God, into a powerful institution that serves the public good and for that reason operates like other social institutions. It transformed servants of the word and the Spirit into professionals, experts with career ambitions. And it converted the Eucharistic table of fellowship into a theater stage where performers can demonstrate their talents and enjoy the spotlight for a few minutes every Sunday. In short, modern churches look very much like worldly institutions that offer opportunities to exercise influence, gain honors, pursue careers, and perform in front of an audience. Should we be surprised that an equal-opportunity society demands that such institutional churches open all offices and functions to women? I hope to reframe the debate by calling into question the institutional-type church, the professional ministry, and theater-style worship. Instead of incorporating women into a flawed system and encouraging them to pursue the same defective values men have pursued for centuries, why not change the system and reform the values?

How to Read this Book

Since none of these disputants speaks for me, you may miss the force of the first three chapters if you read them looking for what Ron Highfield thinks. Also, you will misread the book if you measure the arguments my fictitious speakers make solely by what real-life authors write, because I am not trying to imitate them exactly. Instead, I endeavor to express these viewpoints as a real exponent would *if* they were fully aware of their presuppositions, entirely open about the strengths and weakness of their positions, and completely analytical in their reasoning. My overriding concern is to encourage people to examine these issues in greater depth and with more thoughtfulness than they might otherwise have done. So,

I suggest reading each essay and the responses carefully. Ask yourself about the strengths and weaknesses of each. Allow the conflict of assertions, opinions, arguments, and lines of evidence to discipline your thought to achieve a clearer and more informed opinion. Since I designed this book to help readers seek truth rather than find confirmation, I hope you will work through all the Questions for Discussion at the end of each chapter. Chapter Four makes sense only as a subversive response to the earlier arguments. Read it last.

On Behalf of Secular Feminism
(Taylor George)

I am pleased to be given the opportunity to explain and defend Secular Feminism to this audience. And since you seek clarity in this dialogue, I shall begin with a statement as clear as crystal: *It is wrong everywhere, always, and for everyone to forbid a woman to do something she wants to do solely because she is a woman.* Some things are logically impossible for everyone. No one can be married and single at the same time. Some things are physically impossible for everyone. Flying to the Sun and back cannot be done. The temperature is too great and the gravity too massive. And some things, such as lifting 500 pounds or reciting the Constitution of the United States from memory, are physically possible for some people but not for others. No one should expect to do the impossible, but secular feminists argue that anything that is possible for a woman should also be permissible for her. We recognize as legitimate no law of nature, no social custom, and no human or divine law that forbids women to do what is possible for them. And we condemn every political, social, ecclesiastical, and familial institution that keeps women from actualizing their potential in the way they wish.

Having stated clearly what secular feminists assert, I shall explain the grounds for our assertions. Those grounds fall into two categories. The first concerns a view of the self that is presupposed by all modern progressive movements, including Secular Feminism. The second concerns women's experience of their own selves as women. The modern view of the self began to surface in the Renaissance, advanced in the seventeenth-century Enlightenment and the nineteenth-century Romantic Movement, and came to maturity in the late Twentieth Century. When you disengage the human self from such external frameworks as the state, society, family, church, and nature, which impose on the self a preexisting, unchosen and alien identity, you discover the essential self. This self exists apart from these frameworks and possesses power to create its own identity, that is, to become what it wishes to be. Its one essential property is freedom, the creative power of will. The dignity of the self does not derive from any value system outside the self, from nature or God or society. Its dignity is self-grounded, that is, it is the self's very nature and basic act to value itself, assert its right to determine itself, and liberate itself from all external frameworks and forces. And it demands that others respect its self-respect. This, then, is the first justification for secular feminists' assertion of their right to self-determination against all external frameworks and powers.

The second justification is unique to women. Women are self-creating selves like all human beings but in their own particular way. We secular feminists call it "women's experience." Women experience their female bodies from within, and they experience the external world of nature, society, church, men, and family *as women.* And that experience includes misrepresentation, oppression, exclusion, domination, abuse, and rape. Women's experience includes the feeling of powerlessness, forced silence, and dismissiveness on the part of men. Women experience being valued only for the satisfaction of male lust, as wombs used for reproduction, as housekeepers, cooks, caretakers for children, and babysitters for immature men. Secular feminists consider women's experience an authority by which to critique the oppressive structures of the patriarchal past and those that remain. More precisely, the modern view of the self, which I described above, is the authority by which oppressive structures are judged to be wrong, and women's experience is the way even subtle oppressive structures are revealed as oppressive for women. Because of their experience of oppression, women can see things men cannot see. These two sources together provide a foundation and justification for Secular Feminism.

Now I will detail some practical implications of Secular Feminism. I will be as clear in this section as I was in the first. *Secular feminists demand that every tradition, ideology, theology, or philosophy that justifies male privilege be rejected as false, anti-human, and evil.* We also demand that every framework, order, institution, and structure that inhibits the realization of women's potential be reformed or abolished. These institutions include all public and so-called private institutions: government, churches, military, clubs, families, societies, and schools. And since these institutions are heirs of a long history of oppression, they cannot be left to reform themselves. There must be an aggressive public policy of affirmative action to move rapidly toward equality. As for churches, they are the worst offenders, not only because of their oppressive practices but, more egregiously, because of their patriarchal ideology dictated by the Bible—an ancient misogynous text that ought to have been relegated to the dustbin of failed mythologies long ago, but is still revered by uneducated men and the women they deceive.

Response to Taylor George (Hunter Johnson)

Three Points of Agreement

I'd like to begin my response with the places where I agree with Taylor's presentation. First, in the opening paragraph, Taylor asserts the following principle:

> *It is wrong everywhere, always, and for everyone to forbid a woman to do something she wants to do solely because she is a woman.*

I agree wholeheartedly with this principle. What motivation other than irrational prejudice could anyone have for thinking otherwise? Second, I also agree that women's experience serves as an important source of truth for constructing the ethics of gender relations. Because of their experience of oppression and abuse, women can see oppressive structures and abusive relationships to which men are blind. Even if men come to agree with the principle of equality, they need women to help them see specific areas where they are unjustly privileged. Third, if male privilege is morally wrong, it stands to reason that any theory that justifies it is also morally wrong. Hence, for the most part, evangelical egalitarians agree with Taylor's call for reform:

Secular feminists demand that every tradition, ideology, theology, or philosophy that justifies male privilege be rejected as false, anti-human, and evil.

In sum, as an evangelical equalitarian, I agree with secular feminists when they stand against male privilege, assert the equality of women and call for reform that institutionalizes equality.

Five Points of Disagreement

Despite my agreement with Taylor in certain areas, I am not a secular feminist. And I am grateful for the opportunity to explain why. I am an evangelical Christian. I believe that God is the creator and ruler of all things and that Jesus Christ is Lord and Savior. I don't know whether or not Taylor is an atheist, but it's clear that Taylor leaves God completely out of the theory. Taylor grounds all principles and values in human existence and experience. My specific disagreements with Secular Feminism arise from this fundamental difference. In the following paragraphs, I will address five places where this fundamental disagreement comes to the surface.

As I admitted above, I agree with Taylor on the injustice of rules that keep women from doing what they want to do *just because they are women.* But Taylor goes on to make a much more radical and deeply troubling statement. Taylor says,

> *...secular feminists argue that anything that is possible for a woman should also be permissible for her. We recognize as legitimate no law*

*of nature, no social custom, and no human or
divine law that forbids a woman to do what is
possible for her.*

I understand why Taylor would make this argument. Patriarchal society forbade women to do many things they
were perfectly capable of doing: vote, run marathons, become doctors, serve as police officers, soldiers and fire-
fighters, and to preach in churches. But Taylor goes too
far in saying that whatever is possible should also be permissible. Many immoral, unjust, and illegal things are
possible, but they should not be permitted for women or
men. To free women from rules that derive from the false
idea of male superiority, Taylor denies the legitimacy of
any rule that does not derive from the self-legislating
self, in effect repudiating the objective distinction between right and wrong. This move makes as much sense
as slitting your throat to cure a headache. It's effective,
but the side effects make it impossible to enjoy the cure.
For if there is no objective distinction between right and
wrong, then male domination of women is not objec-
tively wrong either! In contrast to secular feminists,
evangelical egalitarians believe in a God-given moral
law that roots justice, love, and the equality of men and
women in the eternal divine being and will.

My second objection is closely related to the first. It
concerns the source and nature of the dignity of women.
In an astounding claim, Taylor declares,

*The dignity of the [woman's] self does not de-
rive from any value system outside the self,
from nature or God or society. Its dignity is
self-grounded, that is, it is the self's very nature
and basic act to value itself, assert its right to*

17

*determine itself, and liberate itself from all ex-
ternal frameworks and forces. And it demands
that others respect its self-respect.*

This statement contains so many extraordinary claims I hardly know where to begin with my critique. Taylor rejects being created or loved by God as relevant to the dignity of women. Instead of finding dignity in a relationship to God, Taylor grounds it in women's subjective feelings of self-worth. This move allows them to demand that other people make way for them to act as they please and become whatever they wish.

The problem with this view is that our subjective feelings of importance and our desires to live and act as we please cannot justify making objective moral claims on others. Other people have their own feelings and desires that they may assert against our claims. And in Taylor's system, there is no objective arbiter to adjudicate competing claims. Unless human dignity has an objective and universal foundation, it can legitimate no claims against the state, social institutions, or individual human beings. Because there is no universal authority to which all parties can appeal and are willing to submit, efforts at persuasion are doomed to fail, and coercive power becomes the final arbiter between competing wills.

Third, I said above that I agreed substantially with feminism about the importance of women's experience in this discussion. However, Taylor seems to view men wholly negatively. As a Christian, I do not consider men irredeemably evil. Men, too, are made in the image of God. They can repent of their sins, come to know Christ, and learn how to treat women as equals.

My fourth critical observation concerns Taylor's statements about the practical program of Secular Feminism. Taylor says,

> *Secular feminists demand that every tradition, ideology, theology, or philosophy that justifies male privilege be rejected as false, anti-human, and evil. We also demand that every framework, order, institution, and structure that inhibits the realization of women's potential be reformed or abolished...And since these institutions are heirs of a long history of oppression, they cannot be left to reform themselves. There must be an aggressive public policy of affirmative action to move rapidly toward equality.*

While I agree that institutions need to be reformed in an egalitarian direction, I think Taylor's rhetoric labeling patriarchal ideas "false, anti-human, and evil" crosses a line. Such rhetoric seems to arise from deep anger and fuels the fires of hatred. And the obvious willingness to use government coercion to compel the recalcitrant shows that this philosophy of self-assertion, addressed in my second objection, is at bottom an insatiable desire for power that sets itself above the distinctions between good and evil and right and wrong. In its secret heart, it harbors the kind of metaphysical and moral nihilism that would be willing to destroy itself and the whole world to taste one second of revenge on its enemies.

In a fifth objection, I find the assessment of the Bible distinctly uncharitable when Taylor describes it as

*that ancient misogynous text that ought to have
been relegated to the dustbin of failed mythologies long ago but is still revered by uneducated
men and the women they deceive.*

Taylor's disparagement of the Bible and those who love
it betrays a striking lack of empathy for past cultures and
an appalling ignorance of the central message of the Bible. Evangelical egalitarians do not believe the patriarchal aspects of the Bible are essential to its ethics. There
is an internal dialogue within the Bible in which patriarchy is overcome and replaced by equality. We can see
this most clearly in Jesus' teaching and in Galatians
3:26-28, which I will examine further when I present my
defense of Evangelical Egalitarianism:

*[26]So in Christ Jesus you are all children of
God through faith, [27]for all of you who were
baptized into Christ have clothed yourselves
with Christ. [2] There is neither Jew nor Gentile,
neither slave nor free, nor is there male and female, for you are all one in Christ Jesus. [29]If
you belong to Christ, then you are Abraham's
seed, and heirs according to the promise.*

This text shows that evangelical egalitarians have a significant advantage over secular feminists in criticizing
male superiority and advocating the equal dignity of
women. We can ground our program of equality in divine authority. We can challenge Christian men, of
which there are hundreds of millions, to live up to the
ethical demands of their Lord and Savior Jesus Christ.
Secular feminists' assertions of dignity and demands for
respect, once you see through their deceptive rhetorical

form, boil down to expressions of subjective feelings and wishes with no objective authority.

Response to Taylor George (Mackenzie Prestige)

Before I present my analysis of Taylor's essay, I'd like to thank Hunter for a cogent and sometimes brilliant reply to Taylor. Since Hunter and I are both evangelical Christians and share a deep respect for the Scriptures, it won't surprise you to hear that I find myself applauding the five points made in criticism of Secular Feminism. In fact, Hunter did such a fine job in those critiques that I don't need to address them in great detail. However, I find the critique blunted by the three points of agreement with Secular Feminism. Apparently, Hunter thinks you can agree with the basic principle and practical program of Secular Feminism while disagreeing with its theoretical justification for them. I don't believe it is possible to disengage the two so easily. My critique of Taylor's viewpoint will make this plain.

Feminism and the Divinization of Humanity

Hunter really bulls-eyed the target by pointing out that Taylor bases the case for feminism on an arbitrary assertion of power over human existence and action. Since Taylor's whole program centers on liberating the self from all external principles and powers so that it can become and do what it pleases, Taylor has no alternative but to root the "rights," "dignity," and "claims" of women in their own reality. Admitting that the self is responsible to any outside law or power would immediately legitimate a debate about which of its wishes and desires are lawful and good. It would give others—including men—a say in what women do and become. And this is the very intrusion secular feminist theory is designed to exclude.

Hunter critiqued Taylor's theory of the self-creating, self-validating self by reducing it to absurdity and uncovering its secret nihilism. This was a brilliant move. But the theory can also be critiqued from a historical point of view. Taylor presents this absurd view of the self as if it sprang from nowhere and was a matter of self-evident experience. I don't have space here to tell the whole story, but Taylor's view of the self depends on the unacknowledged intersection of two great historical lines of development. They are: (1) *The Christian teaching about human nature and destiny* and (2) *The Christian doctrine of God.* In the history of the Christian doctrines of creation and salvation, it is affirmed again and again that God created human beings in his image and loves each individual. Human beings possess maximum worth or dignity in God's eyes. In God's plan for salvation, human beings will be freed from sin and death and be united to God to live eternally in glory. They will become, as it were, gods. Concerning the doctrine of God, Christianity developed an understanding of divine freedom as God's self-sufficiency, that is, his complete independence from every external power. God is not subject to any law outside his will and being. As one church

24

father put it, God *is* only what he wills to be and *wills* to be only what he is (Gregory of Nyssa, in *Against Eunomius,* 3.6).

Taylor draws on the strand of modern thought that secularized and fused these two histories. It ripped the concept of unlimited human dignity from its Christian matrix and reasoned that unlimited dignity demands unlimited freedom. In a final step, it identified unlimited freedom with complete self-sufficiency and independence from every external power. In other words, Taylor transfers the divine attributes of freedom and self-grounded dignity, developed in the Christian doctrine of God, to the human self. The "image" of God transforms into God himself! Taylor's "woman" demands to be allowed to become only what she wills and insists that her happiness consists in being content with what she is. Taylor's image of woman is a godless goddess who worships and obeys only herself and insists that we also worship and obey her. Viewed against the context of the real human condition, Taylor's theory of the self appears as patently absurd.

All Feminists Together!

Now I will address the three points where Hunter agrees with Taylor. This strategy allows me not only to take advantage of Hunter's excellent analysis of Secular Feminism but also to foreshadow my critique of Evangelical Egalitarianism.

First, Taylor articulates the basic feminist principle in these words:

It is wrong everywhere, always, and for every-one to forbid a woman to do something she wants to do solely because she is a woman.

Hunter can't see anything wrong with this principle, and I would hazard a guess that many of our readers when they heard it simply nodded in approval without a critical thought. Clearly, the qualifying phrase "solely because she is a woman" is the determining factor that elicits the chorus of "Amen! Amen!" to this principle. Why does this assertion seem so beyond dispute? Why does no one even think of questioning it? The reason is simple. And Hunter answers our elicitive question with a rhetorical question, "What motivation other than irrational preju-dice could anyone have for thinking otherwise?" Irra-tional prejudice! Nobody wants to be accused of that!

When we hear the phrase "solely because she is a woman" we analogize it to such phrases as "solely be-cause of the color of his skin" or "solely because she is blond" or "solely because of the size of her nose" or "solely because of his height" or "solely because of her blindness." In these examples, we contemplate a totally irrelevant factor being made the basis for discrimination among people. Its *irrelevant nature* is the reason we view it as irrational. It is irrational to make a decision based on something unrelated to the matter in question. We would not think highly of the intelligence or character of a person who made such life-changing decisions as whom to marry or whether to undergo cancer treatment by flipping a coin!

However, in some situations even such factors as skin color, blondness, nose size, height or blindness may be rationally related to a decision that must be made. Use your imagination! Likewise, being a woman may not always be a factor unrelated to the matter at hand. To say that a particular person is a woman asserts something about her much more significant than skin color or height. Designating a person as a woman says that she possesses a set of specific physical and psychological qualities that differentiate her from men in rather dramatic ways. Clearly, the word "solely" in the phrase *"solely because she is a woman"* is misleading, perhaps intentionally so. There is nothing trivial or superficial about being a woman! Or a man! And because women as a class possess these differentiating qualities, it may be rational, and therefore moral, in some cases *"to forbid a woman to do something she wants to do solely because she is a woman."*

It may be rational, for example, for society to prohibit women from using the same public restrooms as men, playing on the same football team as men, wrestling or boxing on the men's Olympic team, or joining a college fraternity. My point is not that it is *never* irrational prejudice that motivates someone to forbid a woman to do something she wants to do solely because she is a woman. Sadly such prejudice exists. My point is that it is not *always* irrational and prejudiced to do so. Hence societies, churches, and families must deliberate and make decisions about the conditions that make it appropriate to distinguish between the rules for the behavior of men and those for women. These matters cannot be settled in advance by such sweeping rules as the one asserted by Taylor and accepted so unthinking by Hunter.

Now I'd like to turn to Taylor's assertions about male privilege and women's experience.

"Women's Experience"

Taylor asserts that "women's experience" is an authoritative source of truth. According to her, when women feel oppressed and think they are being treated unfairly, men should accept their perspective as a revelation of truth and acquiesce to their demands. Hunter agrees. I disagree. If the subjective feeling of being unjustly treated is a moral norm, why limit it to *women's* experience? Men have experience too! And if women's experience can be used to instruct men about their moral blindness, why can't men's experience instruct women in areas where women are morally blind? If women's experience can refute men's views of women, why can't men's experience refute women's views of men? Why can't men insist that women accept *their* experience as a revelation of truth and demand that women acquiesce to *their* desires?

Unless there is an objective standard of moral truth, justice, and goodness, appeals to experience lead to a stalemate. One person's desires are set against another's with no objective standard by which to judge between them. But if there is an objective moral standard, neither women's experience nor men's experience can be used as a moral norm. At best, they are beginning places for a discussion about how to achieve a mutually acceptable approximation to justice and goodness in this relationship.

"Male Privilege"

Taylor demands that

> ...*every tradition, ideology, theology, or philosophy that justifies male privilege be rejected as false, anti-human, and evil.*

Clearly, Taylor begs the question in this assertion by assuming that "male privilege," that is, giving a right to men that is not given to women, is always wrong. But this is the question to be decided! It cannot be assumed! I can be brief in my response to this assertion because I will argue at length in my presentation of New Complementarianism that in some situations giving men a privilege not given to women is the rational and right thing to do. Hence male privilege is not always wrong! We need to deliberate in society, church, and family about when it is appropriate. There are no easy answers!

One last point. The whole discussion as articulated by Taylor and assumed by Hunter focuses on *male* privilege. What about *female* privilege? Aren't women given some rights withheld from (or irrelevant to) men? Don't women want to be treated differently from men in some cases? But if male privilege is always wrong, female privilege is always wrong as well. Does anyone think women would be better off in a society where they must compete with men under the exact same set of rules?

Questions for Discussion

A. The Feminist Principle

Taylor asserts the feminist principle in these strong words, "It is wrong everywhere, always, and for everyone to forbid a woman to do something she wants to do solely because she is a woman."

1. What are the strengths and weaknesses of Taylor's assertion as a foundational principle for feminism? How would you reformulate it to make it better?

2. Hunter agrees "wholeheartedly" with Taylor's principle. Explain why Hunter is correct or incorrect to accuse anyone who disagrees of "irrational prejudice."

3. What are Mackenzie's criticisms of the feminist principle? Explain why you agree or disagree with the argument that there may be "rational" reasons to override this principle.

B. Self-Grounded Dignity

Taylor grounds the feminist principle and the dignity, rights, and freedom of human beings in the self's own existence and does not appeal to divine law, creation, nature, or culture to justify the claim to self-determination.

1. What is your assessment of the possibility and workability of this assertion?

2. What are Hunter criticisms of Taylor's assertion of self-grounded dignity? Explain why you agree or disagree with Hunter.

3. Explain Mackenzie's contention that Taylor's assertions of complete freedom and self-grounded dignity transfer God's attributes to human beings. Do you agree or disagree? Why?

C. Women's Experience

Taylor argues that "women's experience" of (mostly) oppression and disrespect from men gives women insights unavailable to men and serves as a source of moral truth by which to demand reform of society.

1. Do you agree or disagree with Taylor's characterization of women's experience? To what extent can "woman's experience" be treated as a revelation of moral truth?

2. Hunter agrees "substantially" with Taylor's view of the role women's experience but disagrees with Taylor's wholly negative view of men. Speculate about how Hunter might use "women's experience" in a reform program differently from Taylor's use.

3. Mackenzie offers some sharp criticisms of Taylor's (and Hunter's) argument from women's experience. Discuss Mackenzie's charge that, apart from an objective moral standard, the argument from women's experience is merely subjective and no more authoritative than "men's experience."

D. Secular Feminism's Practical Program

Taylor proposed to reform society, church, and family to rid it of male privilege and establish equality.

1. Explain and evaluate Taylor's purely political approach to reform.

2. Do you agree or disagree with Hunter's criticism of Taylor's willingness to use political coercion to enact the proposed reforms?

3. Mackenzie challenges Taylor's assumption of the pervasiveness and inherent injustice of male privilege and argues that female privilege also exists. And if one is always wrong, so is the other. Does Mackenzie have a point?

E. The Secular Feminist Perspective

1. In what ways did Taylor's presentation of the secular perspective meet your expectations and in what ways did it surprise you?

2. Do you think Taylor's representation of Secular Feminism was fair? Explain your answer.

3. In what ways do you think examining the secular feminist perspective on the issue of women and church leadership adds something of value to this discussion?

In Defense of Evangelical Egalitarianism
(Hunter Johnson)

As became clear in my response to Taylor, I share many concerns, principles, and practical conclusions with Taylor. But we differ in significant ways, and those differences are anticipated by the names of our philosophies.

What is Evangelical Egalitarianism?

Who are evangelical egalitarians, and what do they assert? This school of thought focuses on the concerns of evangelical women, but you don't have to be a woman to be an evangelical egalitarian. The word evangelical derives from the Greek word for good news or gospel. In the English-speaking world, especially in the United States, it has come to mean a trans-denominational theological model with its own style, core beliefs, and practical programs. We believe in Jesus Christ as Savior and Lord, crucified for our sins and raised bodily from the dead. We accept the Old and New Testament Scriptures as the inspired Word of God, the authority for faith and practice for the Christian church. But I am also an *egalitarian,* which many evangelicals are not. Egalitarianism refers to a set of arguments for the equal status (that is, equal in power and privilege) of men and women in society, church, and family. Evangelical egalitarian arguments differ from those of Secular Feminism in that they are primarily biblical and theological. Nevertheless, they arrive at surprisingly similar conclusions.

To those who are wondering why I do not call myself an "evangelical feminist," let me say this. Feminists are a very diverse group. Feminism includes egalitarians but also more radical groups, some of which argue that women must minimize their association with men if they wish to realize their full potential as women. Egalitarians affirm the equal dignity of men and women and do not reject marriage and family. So, egalitarians are feminists of a particular type. But using this term in our self-description would lead to confusion. Evangelical Egalitarianism focuses on the specific project of equalizing the power and privilege of women with that of men in the church and the family.

Principles and Goals

The Feminist Principle

I don't think I could improve on Taylor's first principle, so I shall quote it again as expressing my own thoughts. Taylor and I agree that:

> *It is wrong everywhere, always, and for everyone to forbid a woman to do something she wants to do solely because she is a woman.*

Evangelical egalitarians don't believe that being born a woman is a good reason for society or the church to make rules against engaging in any activity, holding any office, or performing any function. There are, of course, many things that ought to be forbidden—immoral things, such as murder, lying and stealing. And the nature of our mental and physical capacities determines what we are able to do. If you cannot carry a tune, you'll never be an opera star. If you have no capacity for math or logic or creative writing, Harvard won't honor you with a professorship in these areas, whether you are male or female. Evangelical egalitarians do not object to the kind of sorting that works itself out because of the diversity of capacities among human beings. But it is an entirely different thing for an authority such as the state or the church to forbid a woman to do something she has the skill to do solely for the crime of being born a woman. Being female is not in itself a disability or a capacity. So, we condemn such discriminatory prohibitions and call for all rules to apply equally to men and women.

The Biblical Case for Egalitarianism

Now I will address a second issue, the grounds that justify Evangelical Egalitarianism. We do not limit our sources of authority to reason and women's experience as secular feminists do, though we do not reject these sources. They have much to teach. However, we gain access to truth from Scripture that is not available from reason and experience. The Scriptures tell us that God created women and men in his image and that he loves each one of us and wants us to live with him forever. And God demonstrated this love and revealed this purpose by sending Jesus Christ to redeem us from sin and death. Evangelical egalitarians ground the dignity of women and men in the eternal being and will of God, a much more objective, universal, and authoritative foundation than reason and experience alone can provide. Jesus affirmed the dignity of women by accepting them as disciples and treating them with a respect that was considered scandalous in his patriarchal culture.

And Paul's words in Galatians 3:26-29 provide Evangelical Egalitarianism its theme text and interpretative principle by which it measures all other biblical statements about men and women:

> *[26]So in Christ Jesus you are all children of God through faith, [27]for all of you who were baptized into Christ have clothed yourselves with Christ. [2] There is neither Jew nor Gentile, neither slave nor free, nor is there male and female, for you are all one in Christ Jesus. [29]If you belong to Christ, then you are Abraham's seed, and heirs according to the promise.*

I'm not able to document every assertion I am making in this brief statement. Nor can I respond here to every objection I anticipate will be leveled at my viewpoint by Taylor or Mackenzie. But evangelical egalitarians contend that the principles Paul lays down in Galatians 3:28 declare that the social distinctions that determine the way power and privilege are distributed in the world are invalid for the church. And we believe they obligate the church to renounce its traditional practice of withholding certain offices and functions from women solely because they are female.

Without entering into an extensive survey let me remind the reader that the Scriptures provide numerous examples of women prophets, judges, teachers, evangelists, apostles, and preachers. In the Old Testament, we find that Miriam, Moses' sister, is called a prophet (Exodus 15:20). Two chapters of Judges are devoted to the judgeship of Deborah. It is said that she held court and "the Israelites went up to her to have their disputes decided" (Judges 4:5). Huldah's reputation as a prophet was such that the priest Hilkiah and his associates sought an audience with her and reported her prophecies to the king (2 Kings 22:14-20). In the New Testament, we find Junia (a woman) along with Andronicus listed as apostles (Romans 16:7). Women prophets were active in the early church (Acts 21:9; and 1 Corinthians 11:5). Priscilla along with her husband Aquila taught Apollos "the way of the Lord more adequately" (Acts 18:26). Some women (Mary, Lydia, and Nympha) were patrons and overseers of house churches (Acts 12:12; 16:14-15; Colossians 4:15). While it is true that men are more likely than women to hold these offices and perform these functions, these examples demonstrate that women are not, in principle, excluded from them. This fact alone defeats the traditionalist argument that these offices and functions are reserved for men.

Evangelical Egalitarianism's Practical Program

Evangelical Egalitarianism promotes equality for women in all areas of life, but its theological agenda focuses on reforming the discriminatory doctrine and practices of evangelical churches. It contends that decisions about who occupies church offices and performs church functions should be made on the basis of "giftedness" instead of the gender of the gifted person. The Spirit endows women as well as men with wisdom, knowledge, faith, speaking ability, and administrative skill. We call on the church to stop resisting the Spirit's decisions and depriving itself of the gifts God wants to give the body of Christ through its female members. If a woman has the gift of preaching, let her preach. If she can teach, let her teach. If administration is her gift, call her to that work. Let the Spirit decide who should bless the church and how.

Response to Hunter Johnson (Taylor George)

I am a *secular* feminist, and I am skeptical about the existence of God. On the whole, I don't think being religious supports humanistic values or enhances human life. Indeed, I think religion is a dangerous force. It has on rare occasions been harnessed for good, but for the most part, it has not been good for women. This is not the right occasion to make an argument supporting my negative view of religion. I just want the reader to be clear about the position from which I shall evaluate Hunter.

Hunter claims to agree with the feminist principle I stated in my original talk, that is,

> *It is wrong everywhere, always, and for everyone to forbid a woman to do something she wants to do solely because she is a woman.*

And Hunter seems to agree with the practical program of Secular Feminism as well, that is, of reforming every practice that falls short of full equality between men and women. Hunter does not make any rational arguments for the feminist principle and program but seems to accept them as self-evident to any right-thinking and fair-minded person. But then Hunter supplements and supports the feminist principle and program with arguments from the Bible. I am puzzled by this. Why drag the Bible in to support something that is self-evident on the basis of reason and experience? I find this move unnecessary and actually detrimental to the cause of feminism for several reasons I shall explain below.

First, the Bible itself is an object of disagreement and controversy. If the principles and the programs of feminism are self-evident to any right-thinking and fair-minded person, why attempt to support them with arguments from a source that is not self-evidently true and universally held to be authoritative? Hunter claims that the Bible gives evangelical egalitarians moral truth that is not available from reason and experience. As examples of these new truths, Hunter mentions two ideas, that human beings are created in God's image and that they will be raised from the dead to eternal life. It is true that the Bible makes these claims, but they seem to secular feminists unlikely and unknowable. Only someone who accepts the Bible as a divine revelation can take these arguments seriously. What a leap of faith that is! It's not only redundant; it introduces unnecessary ambiguity into the feminist case. It takes the focus off the self-evidence of the moral principle of feminism and places it on the complicated and doubtful process of exegesis and interpretation of the Bible. Hunter's appeal to the Bible actually weakens the case for women's equality! It makes it seem dependent on the improbable theory of divine inspiration.

In the second place, the Bible doesn't teach feminism. When secular feminists read the Bible, they don't hear a message of equality. They hear a message of male privilege and superiority. I think Mackenzie is more realistic and honest about what the Bible actually says than

Hunter is. Hunter attempts to reinterpret the anti-woman passages in ways that subordinate them to the few texts that affirm women in some way. But such interpretative maneuvers seem artificial and complicated. They are unconvincing and give the impression of arising from wishful thinking. The texts are made to say what Hunter already knows to be true from other sources. Hence working so hard to reinterpret the Bible in a feminist direction turns out to be as implausible as it is unnecessary. So what if the Bible teaches male superiority?! Even if it were possible, it's not worth the trouble to retrieve the Bible for feminism. Let it go, Hunter.

Third, using the Bible to support feminism gives the appearance of cynicism. Now I don't wish to question the religious sincerity or conscious motives of all evangelical egalitarians, but I admit that I am somewhat suspicious of their strategy. Why strain so hard to make the Bible into a feminist text? Is it merely because so many people hold it in such high esteem? Is it that Bible believers will never accept feminism unless they can be made to think the Bible supports it…even if it doesn't? Or, is Evangelical Egalitarianism merely a cynical strategy with a purely pragmatic goal? Well, for my part I am fine with cynical strategies. Whatever it takes! But in the long run, people will have to make a choice between the Bible and egalitarianism. They are not compatible.

Fourth, Evangelical Egalitarianism accepts many moral teachings that are incompatible with feminist principles and programs. Hunter claims to accept feminist principles. But the evangelical view of the Bible forces Hunter to argue that some things ought to be forbidden solely because the Bible teaches that they are immoral. Evangelicals hold that non-marital sexual relationships, abortion, gay and lesbian relationships, divorce, and transgender lifestyles are immoral and ought to be forbidden. Many of these moral rules prevent women from exercising moral autonomy and realizing their potential as women. Again, we see how anti-progressive the Bible is.

I conclude that Secular Feminism is a much more efficient route to gender equality than Evangelical Egalitarianism. It doesn't need to apologize for the Bible's retrograde teachings or spend its energy attempting to make the Bible say something it plainly doesn't say.

Response to Hunter Johnson (MacKenzie Prestige)

Let me begin by referring to Taylor's critique of Evangelical Egalitarianism. As a secular feminist, Taylor displays no sympathy for the Bible or evangelical Christianity. But Taylor has stumbled onto the central problem with Hunter's position, that is, the fundamental tension between the Bible's teaching and egalitarianism. Taylor argues for their incompatibility, and so will I. But our agreement ends at this point. Taylor rejects the Bible in order to preserve egalitarianism. I reject egalitarianism in order to preserve evangelical Christianity. And Hunter wants to preserve both.

The Function of the Feminist Principle in Evangelical Egalitarianism

Hunter affirms full agreement with Taylor's feminist principles and programs for reform. For the reader's convenience I will quote Taylor again:

> *It is wrong everywhere, always, and for everyone to forbid a woman to do something she wants to do solely because she is a woman.*

Hunter said of this principle, "I agree wholeheartedly with Taylor. What motivation other than irrational prejudice could anyone have for thinking otherwise?" In my reply to Taylor, I criticized this rule from a rational point of view. I won't repeat those criticisms here except to say that I demonstrated that this principle is neither self-evident nor universally applicable. It is not true that "irrational prejudice" is the only possible motivation for making different rules for men than for women. No one, man or woman, really believes this!

Hunter's larger argument assumes the feminist principle without analysis or argument. It then expends most of its energy attempting to demonstrate that the Bible can be interpreted as supportive of this principle. Clearly, the feminist principle serves Hunter's argument as a self-evident norm by which to measure the moral vision of the Bible. Taylor argued that Hunter's use of the Bible is redundant except as an appeal to the evangelical audience. I think Taylor makes a good point. But if the feminist principle itself is not self-evident and universal, Hunter's entire argument collapses, because the feminist principle serves as a norm that enables egalitarian interpreters to separate the Bible's higher moral vision (egalitarian) from its lower one (patriarchy).

Let's take stock of where we stand. I have made it impossible for Hunter to continue using the feminist principle as an unquestioned norm for biblical interpretation. Even now Hunter's entire argument lies in ruins. It cannot be resurrected without extensive revisions. And without the presumption of the self-evident and universal nature of the feminist principle, the case can never return to its former glory. But now let's look at Hunter's argument from another angle by examining its claim that one can make a strong case for egalitarianism without compromising evangelical Christianity.

Treachery of Feminist Hermeneutics

Hunter claims to be an evangelical Christian and argues that one can defend evangelical theology while affirming the feminist principle. Hunter gives a brief definition of evangelicalism:

> *We believe in Jesus Christ as Savior and Lord, crucified for our sins and raised bodily from the dead. We accept the Old and New Testament Scriptures as the inspired Word of God, the authority for faith and practice for the Christian church.*

Is it possible to reconcile this high view of the Scriptures with egalitarianism? Let me first address Hunter's brief but noteworthy survey of women leaders in the Bible. One could quibble here and there with Hunter's biblical interpretation. Were Andronicus and Junia really outstanding apostles or simply esteemed by the apostles? Interpreters disagree. Mary, Lydia, and Nympha were no doubt patronesses of house churches (Acts 12:12; 16:14-15; Colossians 4:15), but to call them "overseers" of those churches is a stretch. But enough quibbles. Every reader of the Scriptures knows about these texts and admits that women sometimes performed these functions. Who denies this? But Hunter and other egalitarians make an unwarranted leap when they conclude that the Bible's women prophets, apostles, preachers, evangelists, patronesses, and teachers were interchangeable with men prophets, apostles, preachers, evangelists, patrons, and teachers. Women who performed these activities did them *as women,* in a way that befits women. Men performed them *as men,* in a way that befits men. There is no reason to assume that the normal social relations between men and women must be transcended in the exercise of these gifts and functions. Paul's instructions in 1 Corinthians 11, for example, differentiates the conditions under which women are allowed pray and prophesy from those under which men may pray and prophesy.

Of course, Hunter admits that many texts in this "inspired Word of God" fall far short of affirming egalitarianism. In many cases, the Old Testament law makes different rules for men than for women, some of which sound to modern ears highly disparaging to women. Jesus chose only men as apostles. Paul speaks of man as the "head" of woman, and he gives different rules for women and men when they speak in the assembly of the church (1 Corinthians 11:1-16). He tells women to be silent in church and to ask their husbands any questions they have when they return home (1 Corinthians 14:34-38). He speaks of the husband as "the head of the wife as Christ is the head of the church" and enjoins submission of wives to husbands (Ephesians 5:1-21). Peter speaks of woman as "the weaker partner" (1 Peter 3:1-7). In 1 Timothy 2:11-12, women are forbidden to "teach or assume authority over men." The rulers of the church, elders and bishops, must be men (1 Timothy 3 and Titus 1).

Secular or religiously liberal feminists, neither of whom acknowledges the exclusive authority of the Bible for faith and practice, can easily dismiss these texts as products of ancient patriarchy. They don't need the Bible to support their moral vision; they get their morals from progressive culture. But evangelical egalitarians cannot take this easy option. They must find a way to subordinate the "patriarchal" texts to the "egalitarian" ones without denying that Scripture is "the authority for faith and practice for the Christian church." How can this be done?

As I see it, there is only one way. Evangelical egalitarians must argue that the "patriarchal" rules and restrictions on women do not express the essential moral vision of the Bible rooted in the facts of the gospel of Christ. Instead, they need to argue that these regulations are accommodations to patriarchal culture or applications of the principle of 'good order.' Or perhaps, they are 'time-sensitive apostolic judgments,' which can be revised by the church. My concern with this approach to interpreting the Scriptures is this: despite evangelical egalitarian claims to the contrary, many people will conclude that one can remain a good Christian while ignoring or discounting the clear moral teachings of the Scriptures. If we can find a way around the apostolic teaching about the roles of men and women in the governance of the church and the family, what is to keep us following the same procedure when the subject is same-sex marriage or homosexuality or abortion? In other words, I think Evangelical Egalitarianism opens the door to so-called liberal Christianity, which openly rejects the Bible's moral authority and puts personal experience or social consensus in its place.

Galatians 3:28 Again

Hunter and other evangelical egalitarians argue that Galatians 3:28 ("There is neither Jew nor Gentile, neither slave nor free, nor is there male and female.") articulates the essential egalitarian message of the gospel whereas the submission and restriction texts do not. You may be surprised to hear that I agree with Hunter up to a point. In biblical interpretation and doctrinal application it is crucial to distinguish the central gospel message and Jesus' high ethical vision from the particular applications the apostolic church had to make from day to day and situation to situation. Surely everyone knows that Paul would agree that it's much more important to believe the gospel and love your neighbor than to keep women silent in the churches. Is it still important for women to wear a head covering and for men to keep their hair cut short (1 Corinthians 11)? Matters such as these have to be debated and judgments have to be made in every generation. They cannot be settled in advance.

And I agree that Galatians 3:26-29 articulates a central gospel principle:

> *26So in Christ Jesus you are all children of God through faith, 27for all of you who were baptized into Christ have clothed yourselves with Christ. 2 There is neither Jew nor Gentile, neither slave nor free, nor is there male and female, for you are all one in Christ Jesus. 29If you belong to Christ, then you are Abraham's seed, and heirs according to the promise.*

This text states plainly that gender, social status, and ethnic identity do not define one's relationship to God. Faith and baptism unite people to Christ. But evangelical egalitarians are mistaken to use Paul's teaching on justification as proof that all distinctions in society, church, and family should be abolished. Justification deals with something all people share regardless of gender and social standing: all have sinned, and everyone needs a savior. There is no difference. Outside of Christ, everyone is a sinner in need of grace; in Christ, everyone is a sinner saved by grace. But people are not the same in all respects. And Paul and other New Testament authors take these distinctions into account in their moral teaching about social, ecclesiastical, and familial life. And I believe they are right to do so.

Giftedness

Hunter admits that some distinctions must be made in roles, offices, and activities in the church. However, Hunter argues that these differences must be determined by "giftedness" and not by gender. What shall we make of the "giftedness" principle? First, we need to ask about the meaning of "giftedness." In general, it seems to mean a power, native or learned, natural or supernatural, that enables one to perform a task. It's called a "gift" because, whether in a natural way or a supernatural way, this power derives from God and is given by grace. Second, we should observe that to be consistent with the egalitarian assertion, Hunter would have to insist that being created a woman or a man is not a gift. For if our maleness or femaleness were a gift, according to the principle of giftedness, it could rightly become a basis for assigning roles, functions, and offices in the church! But Hunter insists that to be given the characteristics and powers entailed in being a woman or a man implies nothing about participation in church roles, offices, and activities. And for the church to consider maleness or femaleness a gift and make distinctions accordingly would be wrong.

I find Hunter's exclusion of maleness and femaleness from the category of "giftedness" implausible and arbitrary. As I argued in my response to Taylor, being a woman or a man is not a superficial characteristic like eye color or height. The differences between men and women are profound and are bound to have consequences for the order that structures society, church, and home. Hence the apostolic rules differentiating the roles and functions of men and women in the church and home cannot be presumed without examination to be in violation of the Pauline principle of justification by faith or the evangelical egalitarian principle of giftedness.

Questions for Discussion

A. Definition of Evangelical Egalitarianism

Hunter claims to be an *evangelical* egalitarian. Clearly, evangelical commitments both limit and advantage the case for egalitarianism.

1. What are the basic characteristics of Evangelical Egalitarianism?

2. Speculate about the significance of the qualifier "evangelical" in the term "Evangelical Egalitarianism" as opposed to the qualifiers "secular" or "liberal Christian."

B. The Bible and the Feminist Principle

Hunter accepts the basic feminist principle, that is, "It is wrong everywhere, always, and for everyone to forbid a woman to do something she wants to do solely because she is a woman." Moreover, Hunter argues that the Bible not only supports this principle but strengthens the case for its truth.

1. Does Hunter make a good case that the Bible's teaching about human dignity and destiny adds

something significant to the case for egalitarianism?

2. Explain and evaluate Taylor's twin charge that (1) the feminist principle can stand on its own and does not need support from the Bible and (2) that seeking support from the Bible actually weakens the egalitarian case.

3. Evaluate Mackenzie's criticism of Hunter for accepting the feminist principle as a self-evident truth? Do you think Mackenzie's charge that Hunter uses the feminist principle as an interpretive norm to make the Bible conform to egalitarianism is accurate and fair?

C. The Biblical Case for Egalitarianism

Hunter argues that the Bible supports gender equality in church leadership in two ways. First, it portrays women as exercising the same gifts and offices that men exercise. Second, it sets forth principles concerning human dignity, oneness in Christ, and eschatological destiny that make it imperative to work for equality in all aspects of church life.

1. Given the existence of biblical texts and certain theological statements that seem to restrict the place and activities of women in home and church, evaluate Hunter's case that the Bible actually teaches egalitarianism.

2. What is the significance of Taylor's testimony that secular feminists see the Bible as unequivocally

patriarchal and the case for biblical egalitarianism as "wishful thinking"?

3. Do you agree or disagree with Mackenzie's explanation of the cases of women prophets, judges, patrons, and teachers in the Bible, that is, that they conducted these activities "as befits women"?

4. Who has the better interpretation of Galatians 3:26-29, Hunter or Mackenzie? Explain your answer.

D. Giftedness

Hunter argues that gender should not be a factor in choosing those who serve in the offices and carry out the functions of the church. They should be chosen exclusively on the basis of their "giftedness."

1. Do you agree with Hunter that the giftedness of women warrants appointing them to the offices of preaching minister, elder, bishop, and pastor?

2. What do you make of Mackenzie's contention that Hunter's argument about giftedness gratuitously excludes maleness and femaleness from the category of giftedness and Mackenzie's further contention that maleness and femaleness should be recognized as a divine gift that suits one for some tasks and not others?

E. The Evangelical Egalitarian Perspective

1. In what ways did Hunter's presentation of the evangelical egalitarian perspective meet your expectations and in what ways did it surprise you?

2. Do you think Hunter's representation of Evangelical Egalitarianism was fair and representative? Explain your answer.

3. In what ways do you think examining the evangelical egalitarian perspective on the issue of women and church leadership adds something of value to this discussion?

In Defense of New Complementarianism (Mackenzie Prestige)

I am grateful for the opportunity to defend New Complementarianism, the most enlightened and person-affirming of all views of male/female relationships in society, church, and home. Indeed, I am aware that "Complementarianism" is associated in the egalitarian mind with patriarchy, prejudice, and oppression of women. I am not speaking in defense of everyone who calls themselves "complementarian." I am speaking as a *new* complementarian. New Complementarianism maintains the core insight of complementarianism, that is, male leadership in home and church, but places it within an ethical framework grounded in and permeated by the Christian concept of agape love and takes into account the equalizing effects of modern technological advancements. It is important to note at the beginning of my essay that the complementarian viewpoint is not exclusively male. It is advocated by many women as well.

What is New Complementarianism?

New Complementarianism asserts that God created every human being in his image. Each and every person is loved by God beyond all measure, which means that each person's worth to God is incalculable. Men are not worth more to God than women. But we do not conclude from this truth that men and women should be treated equally in every respect. Feminists and egalitarians sometimes fail to notice that equality is a comparative concept. You can love your neighbors equally *even if you do not love them at all!* Equality is a morally neutral term. It belongs in mathematics, not in moral philosophy. It provides little comfort to affirm that God loves everyone equally unless you also specify how much! New complementarians argue instead that God loves each person, male or female, *infinitely.* Hence we place ourselves under obligation to treat women and men according to their infinite dignity. We hold ourselves to higher standards than the ones proposed by Secular Feminism or Evangelical Egalitarianism.

Readers may find themselves confused at this point. Perhaps you expected me to speak like your stereotype of a complementarian. And you may be saying to yourself, "I thought you believed in male superiority and patriarchy." No, I do not believe in male superiority or what you mean by "patriarchy"! And to differentiate myself from those theories I added the adjective "New" to the name of my viewpoint to form the term "New Complementarianism." I can best explain its meaning by examining traditional patriarchy and then differentiating New Complementarianism from it. Traditional patriarchy is a product of reason, common sense, and accumulated experience...with a big dose of sin thrown in. Let's consider patriarchy in its most enlightened form rather than looking for its crudest examples.

In his book *Politics,* Aristotle examines the most basic unit of society, the household. In Aristotle's day, the household was a semi-autonomous sphere headed by the father. The state intruded in its internal affairs only in extreme circumstances. The father could use violence within prescribed limits to enforce obedience on wives, children, and slaves. The ruling order of the household is determined by nature. The natural slave has a strong body but lacks the intelligence and wisdom to rule himself or others. Wives possess the wisdom and intelligence required for ruling but do not possess the strength to rule men, who possess both. The husband possesses both natural strength and wisdom and so is the natural ruler of the household and by extension the city. A wise woman will accept this order and remain soft-spoken to her husband and other men, since it is unwise to rebel against the unchangeable order of nature or provoke fights one cannot win.

In many ways, Aristotle simply states the obvious. Because of their vastly superior intelligence, human beings rule the animal world. Some animals are stronger than human beings, but none possesses comparable intelligence. Ruling requires physical strength and intelligence. Neither alone is sufficient. This is the core truth of patriarchy that New Complementarians accept because it is an indisputable fact. But Aristotle draws a conclusion from these differences that New Complementarians reject. He attributes more natural dignity to men than to women, and he does so because he measures dignity in terms of fitness to rule. Slaves have less, women have more, but men have the most dignity. We reject this formula. As I argued above, the Christian gospel asserts that women and men possess infinite dignity and that men are obligated to treat women in accord with this dignity. And this rule makes all the difference. Men have no right to pursue their needs, desires, or any other private concern at the expense of their wives or other women. Selfishness, male or female, is always wrong. Always!

But how does New Complementarianism incorporate the differences between men and women into its theory? New complementarians insist that we are obligated to love each other and treat each other justly. The concept of justice states that "each receives what he or she is due." But how do we determine what each is due? Egalitarians appeal to the concept of equality to quantify justice. They insist that a just system treats men and women the same. New complementarians appeal instead to the concept of love, that is, each seeks what is truly good for others. We argue that seeking "what is truly good for others" is morally superior to seeking equality of goods and privileges among them. Things can be equally bad for everyone!

Moreover, treating men and women equally in every respect would disadvantage women by validating and institutionalizing the natural advantages men have over women in areas of physical strength and aggressiveness. Women would have to win the goods they enjoy in competition with men on an equal playing field. We do not believe this order would be just, because we define justice in terms of love and not equality. Instead of encouraging men or women to seek "what is truly good for others," such a rule (equal opportunity, same rules), would reward them for pursuing their private interests at the expense of others. Exercising authentic love and justice toward everyone entails uniformly seeking the best for each individual, given their natural and historical circumstances. Insofar as women differ from men, what is best for men may not be best for women.

Allow me to speak briefly as a New Complementarian about how we believe men should treat women. On average, men are physically stronger and more aggressive than women, and they are keenly aware of it. Women are aware of this too, or they should be. Technological advances have lessened but cannot remove the advantage this difference gives men in the contest for power and privilege. Men must decide what to do with this advantage, and there are only two honest options. (The dishonest option is pretending that it does not exist.) A man can use this power to exploit or protect women. We believe the ideology of egalitarianism facilitates exploitation and harms women in the name of helping them. It forces women to compete with men on an equal footing in areas where nature has placed them at a disadvantage. As New Complementarians, we believe that the male form of true love toward women counts every woman as a wife, mother, sister, or daughter. And because wives, mothers, sisters, and daughters are of infinite worth to God, men should determine to use their strength to protect, love, and honor rather than exploit and despise them. We draw our ideals from the original complementarian, the apostle Paul:

> [4]*Love is patient, love is kind. It does not envy, it does not boast, it is not proud.* [5]*It does not dishonor others, it is not self-seeking, it is not easily angered, it keeps no record of wrongs.* [6]*Love does not delight in evil but re-*

joices with the truth. [7]It always protects, always trusts, always hopes, always perseveres (1 Cor 13:4-7).

Principles and Sources of Authority

To what sources does New Complementarianism appeal as justification for its theory and practical program? Like Taylor, I appeal to reason and nature, and like Hunter, I appeal to the Christian Scriptures to support my position. When it comes to moral issues, I believe Christian thinkers like Hunter and I should attempt strenuously to harmonize Scripture, reason, and experience. Sound ethical theories of the relationship between men and women in society, church, and home, must take into account the natural and historical conditions of men and women. Men and women are not equal in every respect. This is a fact of nature. To deny or ignore it is irresponsible and will harm women in the long run. And, as I argued above, egalitarianism ignores the ethical significance of this fact.

Until the resurrection of the dead, where, as Jesus said, people "will neither marry nor be given in marriage; [but] they will be like the angels in heaven" (Mark 12:25; Matthew 22:30), women will live in a world where there are good, weak, and bad men. (There are good, weak, and bad women too, but that is another story.) Any ethical theory of male/female relationships that ignores this reality will inevitably be bad for women. There are a few good men. Good men are aware of their greater physical strength, but they refuse to use it to exploit or harm women. Bad men despise women for being physically weaker and resent them when they excel intellectually. They view women as sex objects to be exploited and weaklings to be bullied. They seduce, intimidate, abuse, rape, and murder women. Weak men lack self-control. They cheat on their wives and refuse to take care of their families; they are lazy, whiny, and resentful of successful women. Good men use their strength to protect women from bad and weak men. And because their self-worth is based on God's judgment, they rejoice in the academic, professional, and other life successes of their wives, mothers, sisters, and daughters.

New complementarians appeal to the Scriptures also. As I argued previously, the Scriptures assert that God created men and women in his image and that God loves both beyond reckoning. The infinite dignity of women is grounded in God's love. And the glorious eschatological destiny of men and women transcends mortal bodily life and the conditions necessary to sustain it. New complementarians believe Galatians 3:26-29 just as strongly as evangelical egalitarians do! Verse 28 asserts, "There is neither Jew nor Gentile, neither slave nor free, nor is there male and female." Being male or female, slave or free, Jew or Gentile is not what counts toward being acceptable to God. What counts is "faith" (v. 26), being "clothed with Christ" (v. 27) and "belonging to Christ" (v. 29). The one thing all Christians have in common is the one thing that matters in relation to God, and it's the one thing that makes us one! This text grounds new complementarians' commitment never to treat a sister (or brother) as inferior.

But Scripture does not draw from this truth the practical conclusion evangelical egalitarians draw, that is, that society, church, and home must create one set of rules that applies to men and women equally. Jesus did not appoint six women and six men to be apostles. When the apostles lost Judas, they selected a replacement from a pool of men only (Acts 1:21-26). The seven "deacons" appointed by the apostles to take care of the Jerusalem church were all men (Acts 6:1-6). Paul gave different instructions for how women and men were to behave in public gatherings of the church. In certain settings, women could "pray and prophesy" as long as they wore a head covering as sign of respect for their husbands (1Corinthians 11:1-16). In other settings, perhaps because of some abuse of speech, women are told to be "silent in the churches" (1Corinthians 14:34-38).

Paul modifies but still uses the traditional Greco-Roman household code to urge women to submit to the rule of their husbands and for husbands to love their wives as Christ loved the church (Ephesians 5:21-31). Peter also adapts the traditional household code, telling women to remain submissive to their husbands and husbands to respect their wives as "the weaker partner and as heirs with you of the gracious gift of life" (1 Peter 3:1-7). In Titus and 1 Timothy, Paul lays down different rules for the behavior of men than those he gives to women. In 1 Timothy 2:11-12, women are forbidden to "teach or assume authority over men." Finally, the rulers of the church, elders, and bishops, must be men (1Timothy 3 and Titus 1).

I am sure Hunter will wish to challenge my use of these texts, and Taylor will view them as manifestations of patriarchal culture to be dismissed summarily. But new complementarians do not believe these texts should be dismissed as benighted or interpreted in a way that makes them irrelevant to our contemporary setting. For sure, allowances must be made for our very different cultures, clothing styles, educational levels, the leveling effect of technology, and more, but nature has not changed. The core insight of patriarchal ethics remains true, that is, since women cannot rule men (except by social convention, a subject for another occasion), the guidelines for the behavior of women must differ in some respects from those governing men. And in a Christian setting, the motivation for the restrictions on the behavior of women, however imperfectly embodied, is protective love, which seeks the best for each person, given their natural and historical circumstances.

Church Leadership Today

What about the contemporary church? Should the church maintain the New Testament's restrictions unchanged? Or should the church, as the evangelical egalitarians insist, erase traditional distinctions? Should it open all offices and functions to women? In contrast to all negative stereotypes, new complementarians do not mindlessly wish to preserve role differentiations solely because they are traditional and made sense in the past. We believe Scripture's restrictions were intended for the good of women and men and for the welfare of the whole church. They were designed to affirm the goodness of the created differences between male and female, to protect women from bad men, and to keep the ecclesial order aligned with the natural family order. And we believe these truths and goals are just as important and obligatory today as they were in the First Century.

Women are not the natural rulers of men. Men know this, and women know it too. Hence the church must maintain some form of role differentiation to make sure that the church's social order does not contradict the natural, created family order. To be specific, we don't think women should be appointed to ruling offices, whatever those happen to be in your denomination, for example, preaching minister, priest, pastor, executive minister, bishop, or elder. The church maintains these distinctions for the sake of true love and enlightened justice, for men and women. For nothing but sorrow and pain can come from fighting against the Creator and the created order. But the exact shape of the ecclesial order must work itself out over time.

Response to Mackenzie Prestige (Taylor George)

There are so many things I'd like to address in Mackenzie's talk, its mood of condescension, its male-normative perspective, and its exaggeration of female vulnerability. My suspicion is that Mackenzie's rational and theological arguments are mere rationalizations of the prejudices I just mentioned. I will let the reader decide. Despite these suspicions, I will keep my assessment of Mackenzie's talk focused on its philosophical aspects.

As I see it, Mackenzie's case rests on a rational analysis of the natural characteristics of women and men. Men are physically stronger and temperamentally more aggressive than women. Women become pregnant, carry babies, and provide them with milk from their bodies. These factors make women vulnerable to male exploitation and dependent on male protection. According to Mackenzie, these facts of nature will necessarily manifest themselves at the social level, and consequently, they justify the social, ecclesial, and familial inequities present in traditional societies. To be fair, I should point out that Mackenzie admits that particular arrangements will differ from society to society and from age to age. Nevertheless, it is clear that Mackenzie denies that these natural inequalities will ever be neutralized completely at the social level. Nor should they be, in Mackenzie's view.

Far be it from me to deny the basic facts of biology. Nor do I deny that biological differences will manifest themselves in society. In a one-on-one, unarmed encounter, men have the advantage over women in a fight to the death. In primitive, warrior societies where the survival of the tribe depends on its effectiveness in battle, I admit there are good reasons for the traditional division of labor between men and women. And I understand that the warrior class (males only) will also demand to be the tribal leaders. Nor do I dispute the overall reasonableness of this demand, since leadership in that setting consists in conducting war or perpetually preparing for it.

Like Aristotle, Mackenzie recognizes that women and men are on average equal in native intelligence. I think Mackenzie would also admit that if human minds did not live in bodies or if they could be transferred to unisex humanoid robots, the differences would be overcome. So far so good, but our agreement ends here. From this point on Mackenzie's argument goes terribly wrong. The facts do not warrant the conclusions drawn from them. Though modern technology has made the physical differences between men and women far less significant in the sphere of work and war than in the past, Mackenzie still seems to think that the superiority of the naked male body for war and work (hard physical labor) creates a moral imperative for society to mirror this relationship of superiority and inferiority in all dimensions. Perhaps the belief that God created nature lies behind the assertion that the order of nature possesses the force of law. Some such metaphysical belief must be at work here.

I begin at a different place and argue for a different result. I argue that equality of intelligence between men and women, which Mackenzie also accepts, creates a moral imperative for us to strive for equality in all other areas. Biology should not determine ethics. Or, as one of my feminist mentors said, "Biology is not destiny!" Unlike Mackenzie, I do not believe in divine creation. Evolution creates facts but imposes no moral obligations. Hence I do not believe that the factual biological order possesses any moral force. In sum, Mackenzie allows biological inequality to blunt the moral force of intellectual equality. I argue that it should be the other way around. I envision a society where technology has made nearly all work depend on knowledge rather than muscle, thought instead of testosterone, and where law roots out all irrational bias against female workers. As to areas of work where muscle still determines productivity, I believe society should not allow profit to be the sole determining factor for allocating social goods. The moral imperative of intellectual and moral equality should exclude any bias against women in hiring for such labor-intensive jobs.

Concerning Mackenzie's contention that women continue to need male protection, it should be pointed out that everyone, men as well as women, needs police protection against violent criminals, male or female. Men murder other men more often than men murder women. Society as a collective is neither male nor female, and it is stronger than any one man or gang of men. Society has replaced big brothers and fathers as the protector of women. Modern family law has replaced the will of father as the law of the household and has outlawed domestic violence, marital rape, and other abuses of women.

In response to Mackenzie's theological arguments, I have little to add to my case against Hunter's theological use of the Bible. In response to Hunter, I argued that the Bible cannot be made to support feminism; such support would be redundant in any case. Feminism doesn't need any help from religion. Indeed, Mackenzie represents the Bible more accurately than Hunter does. Hunter is grasping at straws. Mackenzie is correct to argue that the Bible supports patriarchy, or in Mackenzie's terms "complementarianism," rather than egalitarianism. But I am not moved by either argument, for the Bible holds no authority for me. The arguments between Hunter and Mackenzie about biblical interpretation seem to me much ado about nothing.

Response to Mackenzie Prestige (Hunter Johnson)

At the close of our debate, I'd like to thank Taylor and Mackenzie for their stimulating presentations and incisive responses. From my perspective, among the most interesting and surprising developments in these discussions were those occasions where Taylor and I agreed against Mackenzie or Mackenzie and Taylor agreed against me or Mackenzie and I agreed against Taylor. I didn't expect these strange alliances to develop. Each person's presence added something important to the discussion. And I have to say, I found both my dialogue partners' thoughts challenging. Taylor challenged me to show more convincingly just how the message of Scripture supports the case for equality in ways reason and experience cannot. Mackenzie's creative use of reason and Scripture to support the justice of traditional role differentiation surprised me and made it necessary for me to seek in the future a combination of the two that supports egalitarianism. But for now, I must content myself with replying to the central argument in Mackenzie's presentation.

The Argument for New Complementarianism Summarized

As I understand it, Mackenzie's argument can be summarized as follows: Mackenzie asserts the infinite worth of each individual, man or woman, and insists that our primary duty to one another is love, which is defined in this way:

To love another is to seek what is best for them individually, given their natural and historical circumstances.

Hence to love others and do them justice cannot be identified with treating them equally but falls under the rule of seeking "what is best" for each person. Mackenzie argues further that since men are on average much stronger physically and more aggressive in temperament than women, the rule of love and justice—that is, of "seeking what is best"— demands that men adopt an attitude of protectiveness toward women. In a just order, the rules and roles for women must give them special protections not needed by men. In Mackenzie's words,

New Complementarians believe they ought to view women as mothers, wives, sisters, or daughters and adopt a loving and protective attitude toward all women. Not a condescending attitude, for we know that women are just as intelligent and wise as men and women possess infinite worth to God.

Based on this moral vision, Mackenzie criticizes the egalitarian demand that all social functions and church offices and roles be open to women and men alike based on giftedness (or ability) rather than on gender. Instead of this meritocratic rule, Mackenzie defends the church's traditional practice of withholding "ruling" offices and functions from women as consistent with the teaching of Scripture and the demands of love and justice as exemplified by Jesus.

Four-Part Response

What's Wrong With Equality?

In criticizing my emphasis on equality, Mackenzie asserts that women and men possess infinite worth in God's eyes. Equality, however, is a morally suspect idea. Apparently, Mackenzie thinks my argument and practical program for reform depend on the concept of equality. Without it, egalitarianism falls to the ground. In response, I admit that attributing infinite worth to women says something more sublime about women than the equality claim asserts. But if both men and women have "infinite" worth, don't they also have *equal* worth? So, how does Mackenzie's move defeat my argument? Shouldn't women still be treated equally even within Mackenzie's theoretical framework? How can anyone justify departing from the rule that equal dignity demands equal treatment?

Mackenzie replies to the equal-dignity-equal-treatment challenge by defining love and justice as "seeking what is best" for each person, given their natural and individual differences. Infinite dignity demands not equal treatment but true love and justice individualized for the needs of each person. It's hard to find anything wrong with this principle in theory. But here is the problem: who decides "what is best" for men and women collectively or individually? Wouldn't there be lots of room for stereotypes, misinformation, prejudice, and selfishness in such deliberations? And why should men have any say in determining "what is best" for women? Perhaps each woman should decide for herself what is best for her?

To escape this endless, convoluted discussion, evangelical egalitarians choose equality as the norm for the treatment of women rather than "what is best." The concept of equality is simple and generates simple rules. It's not subject to endless discussions that attempt to take into account myriads of factors. Indeed, as Mackenzie points out, equality is more a mathematical than a moral concept. But at least mathematics is simple! There is less room for obfuscation and humbug!

Even for Christians, "Biology is not Destiny!"

Mackenzie makes much of the biological differences between men and women. I grant that in raw physical strength and psychological aggressiveness men have a natural advantage. But Mackenzie argues that those biological differences demand to be embodied in hierarchical relationships in society and church. Though technological advances can ameliorate the social impact of these differences to some extent, they cannot neutralize them completely. Taylor dealt with this claim effectively in response to Mackenzie, so I don't need to address it at great length. However, I want to consider one aspect that Taylor as a secular person could not really understand or deal with effectively. Taylor pointed out that Mackenzie presupposes that God's choice to create male and female unequal in the areas mentioned above justifies maintaining traditional social inequities. Taylor deals with the problem by dismissing divine creation. I do not believe this is necessary. Indeed, as an evangelical Christian, I believe God created male and female with all the differences this entails. Those differences are good for each gender and for society. We are better and happier together than alone. But it does not follow that it is wrong to strive to overcome the negative impact of those differences, especially when they are magnified by the effects of sin. God also made males and females intelligent, so it cannot be wrong to use this God-given intelligence to equalize the sexes in the workplace and other areas. If it were wrong to use our intelligence for this purpose, wouldn't it also be wrong to use it to cure diseases, treat pain, increase productivity, and enhance human life? Even for Christians, "Biology is not destiny!"

Condescension and False Dichotomies

Mackenzie argues that men will relate to women either protectively or exploitatively, allowing no third alternative. As Mackenzie sees it, on average men possess a superior physical strength of a kind that gives them the ability to intimidate and harm women in one-on-one, private encounters. This fact forces men, whether consciously or not, to adopt one of two attitudes toward women: protectiveness or exploitativeness. Although Mackenzie asserts that protectiveness need not be "condescending," I am not convinced of this. It seems to me that both protection and exploitation are condescending and domineering. Both imply that women depend on the goodwill of men in ways that men don't depend on the goodwill of women. These attitudes discount the equal dignity and intelligence of women and reduce them to their bodies. And this condescension is a constant source of insult and irritation to women. I don't deny the biological facts of the situation, but why can't men overcome the impulse to condescension of any kind and simply treat women as equals? Why must the issues of sex and power—as inseparable as the two sides of a coin—cast their cold shadows over every encounter between men and women?

The Weakness of the Biblical Case for New Complementarianism

What about the teaching of Scripture? Mackenzie contends that Scripture teaches the subordination of wives to husbands in the home and of women to men in the church. Can Scripture really be defended from the secular feminist charge of irrational male prejudice by showing that Scripture's perspective and its instructions are reasonable, just and loving when measured against the facts of nature? And Mackenzie anticipates the evangelical egalitarian argument from Galatians 3:26-29 ("There is neither Jew nor Gentile, neither slave nor free, nor is there male and female.") by limiting its application to justification by faith. In Mackenzie's interpretation, these verses speak exclusively of a new way of relating to God. In the matter of sin and forgiveness, the worldly status of people makes no difference. All that counts is faith and the life that flows from it. This text does not speak of actually recreating people so that they are no longer male and female. Hence, according to Mackenzie, we should not take it to imply that the traditional social, ecclesiastical, and familial orders should be reordered so that being male or female makes no difference. Therefore reserving the "ruling" offices in the church for men is not only reasonable, just and loving, but also obligatory. I shall reply to each phase of this argument in order.

First, in his use of reason and natural law to absolve Scripture of irrationality and male bias, Mackenzie presents an interesting case for New Complementarianism. Some people may find it compelling. But I don't believe it really meets the challenge of Secular Feminism. It leaves the essential idea of patriarchy intact. I also want to defeat those critics of Scripture who accuse it of such prejudice. But I don't see the need to appeal to biology and natural law. I think we can demonstrate that the central message of God's love and the new creation in Christ shows that patriarchy, new or old, is peripheral to the ethics of Scripture and has been made obsolete by the Christian vision of equality in Christ.

Second, I've already dealt extensively with Galatians 3:26-29 in this dialogue, so I don't need to spend much time on it here. I admit that the subject of this text is justification before God and unity in Christ. This is the subject under discussion in the Galatians as a whole. But that doesn't settle the issue of what follows from the fact of our solidarity in Christ. If our worldly status makes no difference in the matter of sin and salvation, surely we who know this are not permitted to carry on "business as usual" in society, church, and family! If God accepts us because of our faith rather than our biological or social status, surely we must accept and relate to each other on this same basis! And if we really accept each other on this basis, how can we defend an order based on biological and social status? Moreover, if we insist on continuing the old order, don't we render our assertions of salvation by faith and oneness in Christ empty phrases? Pious platitudes with no ethical teeth?

Third, what is this talk about "ruling" and "ruling offices" in the church? Jesus rebuked his disciples for talking like this. He told them that the greatest among them is the one who serves all the rest (Mark 9:33-37). And Jesus himself set the example of greatness in service by washing his disciples' dirty feet and dying on the cross (John 13:1-17 and Philippians 2:1-11). The New Testament understands every office and every function in the church as service to others for Christ's sake. If we are thinking rightly about church offices and functions, we will view them as *serving activities, not as ruling activities.* Hence even if you think women should not *rule* over men, why object to them serving the church in any way they can and doing anything the church needs done and calls them to do?

Questions for Discussion

A. New Complementarianism on Equality and Agape

Mackenzie argues that egalitarianism is mistaken to equate justice with equality. Equality is a lesser ideal than agape love. Besides, treating everyone equality will lead to injustice. Instead, we ought to seek what is truly good for each person, given their natural and historical circumstances. Hence treating people unequally is often demanded by true love and authentic justice. For treating them unequally is sometimes the only way to treat them as equals.

1. Discuss the strengths and weaknesses of Mackenzie's analysis of equality, justice, and agape love.

2. Is Hunter's critique of Mackenzie's view of equality and love effective? What are its strengths and weaknesses?

B. Aristotle, Biology, and Leadership

Mackenzie's argument relies heavily on the biological and psychological differences between men and women. Men and women are equal in intelligence but unequal in physical strength and psychological aggressiveness. Men are the natural protectors of women and the community as a whole. Hence the New Testament church and traditional churches of more recent generations were not necessarily being irrational and misogynous when they assigned different roles and functions to women than those they assigned to men.

1. What do you make of Taylor's response to Mackenzie's argument from biology, that is, the argument that intellectual equality should trump inequality in physical strength?

2. What are the strengths and weaknesses of Hunter's argument that, since God created men and women equal in dignity, Christians ought to do everything within their intellectual power to neutralize the negative effects of the areas of natural inequality?

C. The Good/Bad Man Argument

Mackenzie argues that the male's superior strength and greater aggressiveness places him in a position to choose between two identities: protector or exploiter. A bad man will exploit women. A good man will love and protect women.

1. Do you agree with Mackenzie? Explain why or why not.

2. Taylor admits that the biological differences between men and women put women at a disadvantage in some situations but argues that Mackenzie exaggerates those disadvantages and that they

can be all but neutralized by modern technology. Do you agree or disagree with Taylor?

3. Hunter senses an attitude of condescension in Mackenzie's description of the good man and denies that men have only two choices. Discuss the merits of Hunter's reply.

D. The Biblical Case for New Complementarianism

Mackenzie argues that the biblical case for New Complementarianism is overwhelming and that efforts to reinterpret the Bible as teaching egalitarianism are strained at best. The only way out for egalitarian interpreters is to argue from the principles of the New Testament against the practices of the New Testament. The classic case of this failed strategy is the egalitarian argument from Galatians 3:26-29.

1. Has Mackenzie succeeded in demonstrating the ineradicable complementarian nature of the New Testament order? Or, is Hunter correct that "patriarchy" is peripheral to the main biblical message of equality?

2. Did Hunter succeed in rebutting Mackenzie's criticism of the egalitarian interpretation of Galatians 3:26-29?

E. Church Order Today

Mackenzie argues that the ruling offices and functions in the church should be reserved for men. Since women are not the natural rulers of men and since the New Testament church reserved the ruling offices for men, the church of today should maintain the New Testament practice. Scripture, reason, and tradition agree in this matter. Egalitarianism ignores or rejects these authorities and replaces them with the spirit of the times inspired by the modern understanding of the self as autonomous and disembodied.

1. What are the strengths and weaknesses of Mackenzie's practical conclusions?

2. Does Hunter make an effective argument against Mackenzie's practical program by appealing to Jesus' rejection of the worldly conception of "ruling"? Does it make the difference Hunter says it does to consider the offices of preaching minister, elder, and bishop as *serving* functions instead of *ruling* functions?

F. The New Complementarian Perspective

1. In what ways did Mackenzie's presentation of the new complementarian perspective meet your expectations and in what ways did it surprise you?

2. Do you think Mackenzie's representation of New Complementarianism was fair and representative? Explain your answer.

3. In what ways do you think examining the new complementarian perspective on the issue of women and church leadership adds something of value to this discussion?

On Behalf of a More Excellent Way

As I indicated in the Introduction, I am not publishing this book to argue for a particular viewpoint about women's roles and leadership in institutional churches and the professional clergy. I don't defend a particular practical program for every church. Each congregation, each set of church leaders and, indeed, each Christian must come to their own conclusions and implement their own solutions to the challenges they face. But I believe the conversations among the three disputants in this debate clarify many of the challenges facing the church about this issue. In the following paragraphs, I want to address the challenges. Afterward, I will present my proposal for "a more excellent way."

The Challenge for Evangelical Egalitarian Movement

For those who want the church to embrace the equality of women's participation in its life, offices, and functions, the challenge will be finding a way to justify this move while:

1. rejecting unambiguously modern progressive culture's view of the self,

2. maintaining Christianity's view of divine creation and its definition of a good human life, and

3. preserving the authority of the Scriptures for faith and practice.

I do not argue that this feat is impossible. But I think this book shows that it will be difficult to achieve, and it will require much more and much deeper theological reflection than I have seen so far from egalitarians. The vulnerability of Evangelical Egalitarianism on this front was exposed from the left by Taylor and from the right by Mackenzie. Making the case that Scripture actually teaches egalitarianism will be no easy task, because such an interpretation contradicts the clear instructions of some New Testament texts and the near universal interpretation of the historic church. Moreover, can evangelical egalitarians escape the charge made by Taylor and Mackenzie that they secretly rely on progressive culture's view of the self for their interpretation of Scripture? Or, is the modern autonomous self the real driving force for their theory and practice?

The Challenge for Traditionalists

For those who, in the face of the demands of progressive culture, wish to reassert the New Testament texts that restrict women's roles, the challenge will be answering the objections of many Christians who instinctively feel that these restrictions codify injustice, cut against their lived experience, violate the true spirit of Christianity, and derive from irrational male prejudice. I believe traditionalists must face the following question: Is it enough to assert that the Scriptures forbid women to hold the ruling offices of preacher, pastor, elder, and bishop without also demonstrating why these restrictions are rational, loving, and in keeping with the highest spirit of Christianity? In my view, to meet this challenge, traditionalists must overcome the tendency to view the New Testament's moral teachings as isolated commands and, instead, work toward grasping the inner coherence of the Christian moral vision. Without giving up their convictions on the subject of women's roles, they need to distinguish clearly between time-bound customs and the perennial moral teaching in the New Testament. It would advance their cause if traditionalists would study the philosophical foundations of the culture to which the modern vision of the self is so powerful and alluring. I also think traditionalists need to consider whether it is possible to make some adjustments in the roles women play in the work of church without compromising the Christian vision of creation, jettisoning the authority of Scripture, or giving plausibility to the progressive view of the self-creating self.

A More Excellent Way

I've been thinking about the issue of women and church leadership for at least forty years. I've found myself on both sides of the debate but never fully satisfied with my answer. I think I've discovered why. Until quite recently, I accepted without question the usual terms of the debate.

I thought the discussion had to be about whether women could enjoy the same privileges men enjoy in leading *institutional churches.* May women join the professional clergy? May they preach and administer the sacraments? May they become bishops and elders? I never considered that the institutional form of the church was the root cause of the problem, that is, that the coveted "privileges" desired by women exist only because we've replaced the New Testament church with a social institution modeled on worldly patterns. In this chapter, I want to share my discovery for the first time.

The "Benedict Option"

In his recent book, *The Benedict Option: A Strategy for Christians in a Post-Christian Nation* (New York: Sentinel, 2017), Rod Dreher draws a parallel between the cultural situation faced by Benedict of Nursia in sixth-century Italy and our situation today in the western world. Benedict found his culture so morally corrupt and inhospitable to authentic Christian living that he withdrew from society and eventually founded the Benedictine order of monks. The social fabric of Benedict's day was being ripped apart by barbarian tribes waging constant war to expand their domains. Our barbarians, says Dreher, don't wear animal skins or overrun neighboring tribes. They wear designer suits and use smartphones, but they are just as dangerous to authentic Christian living as their sixth-century counterparts: "They are at work demolishing the faith, the family, gender, even what it means to be human" (p. 17), and they call such work "progress."

We live in an increasingly secular culture, and the minute we step outside the church door we are faced with enormous pressure to conform to the progressive vision of human life or at least to remain silent in our dissent. It is becoming ever more difficult for serious Christians to engage in such professions as public school teaching, the professorate, or medicine. And ever-expanding antidiscrimination laws make engaging in businesses such as the florist trade, catering, and photography risky for conscientious believers. The culture war is over, declares Dreher; Christians lost, the barbarians won. The public square has officially become a secular space and hostile territory.

In response to this new situation Dreher urges Christians to distance themselves from the dominant culture to form Christian countercultures. Leave public schools and form classical Christian schools or homeschools, don't idolize university education, consider learning a trade, make your churches real communities that support authentic Christian faith and life (at whatever cost), turn off the television, wean yourself away from social media, and "turn your home into a domestic monastery" (p. 124). It's a radical vision, I know, and many will dismiss it as apocalyptic. However, those who long for a social space to live an authentic Christian life with their families and like-minded Christians may find in Dreher's vision of the "Benedict option" an inspiration to take action.

How do Dreher's cultural analysis and his "Benedict option" shed light on the question addressed in this book? In my view, Dreher helps us reframe the issue in a radical way. He compels us to ask a more fundamental question than the one posed in the subtitle of this book:

"Should Bible-Believing (Evangelical) Churches Appoint Women Preachers, Pastors, Elders and Bishops?" This original question presupposes a certain view of the church and its relationship to secular culture that "the Benedict option" calls into question. The more fundamental issue is this: "How much of the controversy about women's roles in church leadership have we brought unnecessarily upon ourselves by

1. changing the church from an extended family whose sole purpose is to serve God into an institution that serves the public good and for that reason operates like other modern social institutions,

2. transforming ministry in the church into a profession, a career requiring graduate education, and

3. transmuting the Eucharistic table of fellowship into a theater stage?"

The Church as a Social Institution

In friendlier times the church was considered by the broader culture a social institution deserving recognition because of its contribution to the common good. Forming God-fearing, church-going, family-establishing citizens was considered a service to the nation. Traditional marriage, self-discipline, and work were considered social goods. But we no longer live in friendly times, and the definition of "the common good" has changed dramatically. It now includes the ideologies of pluralism and multiculturalism, sexual license, expanded definitions of the family, gender fluidity, and abortion. In certain influential sectors of culture the church is viewed as

a powerful and stubborn preserve of superstition and reactionary morality. Through a combination of entice-
ment, intimidation, and persuasion, mainstream culture
attempts to move the church into conformity with its
moral standards and social goals. And its tactics are
meeting with stunning success.

Especially after the American Civil War, many American denominations also came to think of themselves as
social institutions and touted their contributions to society. Some churches even made social utility their main—
if not sole—reason to exist. Most churches take for
granted such social privileges as tax-exempt status and
the right to own property. They value social approval and
visibility. Sadly, it is becoming apparent that the
church's unspoken agreement with society was a deal
with the devil. For if a church presents itself to the public
as a social institution, valuable because of its contributions to the common good, can it complain when the public comes to expect it to behave like other social institutions?

But the greatest danger to the Christian identity of
churches doesn't come from outside the gates; home-
grown "barbarians" are working from inside. Churches
that sacrifice discipline and orthodoxy to pursue growth,
popularity, and social influence will find themselves
mortgaged to the world. And those mortgages will eventually come due. Should we be surprised when church
members and clergy who have marinated in progressive
culture their whole lives press their churches to conform
to that culture? Can the church retain its Christian identity while also clinging to its political privileges, social
approval, and community visibility? Pursuing something
like "the Benedict option" may soon become the only

way we can live authentic Christian lives in modern culture. Perhaps that time has already come.

In facing the challenges our secular culture presents, it will be helpful to remember that Jesus Christ did not found the church to serve society and authentic Christianity cares little for secular definitions of the common good. It is not intrinsically wrong for the church to use what advantages a society may grant. But it should always keep clearly in mind that it does not need to own property, employ clergy, and enjoy tax-exempt status in order to exist in its fullness. It does not need political influence, social respectability, or community visibility. It does not even need legal recognition. The church can get along quite well without these "privileges" (It did so for centuries, and still does in some areas of the world). There may soon come a time when retaining its privileges at the cost of its Christian identity will become its greatest temptation. And it will fall unless it remembers that its one and only purpose is to serve its Lord whatever the cost.

A Church of Experts and Bureaucrats

Most institutions in modern society have become highly rationalized and bureaucratized. Such institutions operate according to rules that rationalize the means by which they achieve their goals, and the function of the proverbially myopic bureaucrat is to obey the rules given from above and enforce the rules on those below. In such institutions, relationships are depersonalized and people become functions. Whether the functionary is a man or woman makes less difference than in systems that depend on personal relationships for their proper functioning. In a bureaucratic organization, respect is generalized to mean respect for the system and its rules.

As we see clearly in the New Testament, the first churches were not highly rationalized and bureaucratized as are modern institutions. They were organized as extended families, and they retained a close link to the family model of order and authority. Appointment to an office merely formalized the existing respect and admiration of the community for an individual. It did not bestow authority where none was previously present. In contrast, a bureaucrat's authority resides wholly in the office held. Passing over many centuries of change in the institutional forms of the church, contemporary churches find themselves attempting to carry on church life with an order that mixes the rationalization and bureaucratization of a modern institution with the natural family order of the earliest church. And here, perhaps, is the origin of much of our confusion and disagreement. If preaching and leading a church are purely bureaucratic and expert functions, gender makes no difference. Continuing to enforce a set of rules derived from the natural family on bureaucratic institutions makes no sense in terms of the logic of such institutions. Hence the most urgent question we face today is not whether the institutional church should appoint women preachers, bishops, and elders. The question is whether we have the courage to rid ourselves of the bureaucratic institutions we call churches and restore the early church's model of life and order.

The Professionalized Ministry

Another complicating factor is the professionalization of the ministry. When serving the church becomes a profession, the ministry becomes a prize to be sought for the public recognition and honor it promises. It becomes a pathway to personal fulfillment and a means of livelihood. And if the functions of preaching, teaching, and leading a church are merely expert functions requiring only native talent and appropriate training, it seems irrational and unfair to prohibit women from assuming these offices and performing these duties. It makes sense to ask why these prestigious and fulfilling jobs should not be available to those women who are able and prepared to do them. Perhaps this is so. But shouldn't we ask the prior question about whether the church should *have* a professionalized ministry? Would a church without paid, professional clergy *need* to discuss whether to hire a woman minister?

From Fellowship Table to Theater Stage

In the first-century church, people gathered in a house around a family table to share a meal and eat the Lord's Supper. It was in this context that they read the Scriptures, prayed, and encouraged each other. The issues that concerned Paul in 1 Corinthians 11 and 14 focused on women behaving in the gathering of the church in ways they would not have behaved in their own households and thus shaming their husbands in public. The places we gather and the way we conduct our services differ dramatically from those first gatherings and have transformed the meaning of the assembly. They have also had a significant impact on how we approach the issue of women in leadership. Most believers meet in "auditoriums" where the "audience" faces a focal point, a stage where people with microphones speak or sing or play. The question arises about who gets to stand in this place of honor. Leadership becomes largely synonymous with a visible and audible presence on stage. The architectural form of the meeting place exercises a decisive influence on the meaning of the activities that take place there. Our church buildings resemble other public buildings, such as theaters, law courts, university classrooms, and legislative chambers, where contemporary women speak freely and with authority. In contrast, even a contemporary gathering of friends in a house to share a meal, participate in the Supper, and engage in holy conversation still retains the feel of a family gathering. The ethic of the family provides the order: fathers, mothers, children, and friends. Professional entertainers, orators, after-dinner speakers, and business managers would be out of place. My guess is that for most contemporary household gatherings of Christians, Paul's instructions to the Corinthians would still feel appropriate.

Imagine a Different Order

What if the church were still a family that met around a table to share the Supper, to pray for each other, and listen to the Scriptures read? And what if the church's ministers were those who served without pay and its leaders were those whom the people felt compelled to follow because of the authority of their lives? And what if there were no theater, no stage, and no microphone? Would we be discussing the issue of women in leadership? Would churches be divided into egalitarians and complementarians? I am not arguing that returning to the New Testament model is the only viable solution to the question discussed in this book, though I believe it is the best solution. It is unrealistic to expect Christians to dismantle the entire structure of traditional churches in favor of house churches, but for my part, I am weary of institutional, bureaucratic churches and want to see more house churches established according to the New Testament model.

Of course, there are disadvantages as well as advantages to such a shift. And historically there were good reasons, as well as bad ones, for institutionalization. My hopes are modest. My hope is that traditional churches will offer greater resistance to the logic of bureaucracy, reverse the trend toward professionalization of the ministry, abandon the theater model of the assembly, and find creative ways to get closer to the New Testament model. It would be too optimistic to think that carrying out such reforms would completely resolve the issue of women in church leadership. But shattering the analogy between the church and secular social institutions might remove some of the less noble motivations—recognition, professional advancement, money, visibility, and power—for aspiring to leadership in the church. We might actually have some productive discussions about how each part of the body can use the gifts God has given to benefit the whole church. And we might find greater joy in our friendship and fellowship, since we would spend less emotional energy in possessiveness or envy over who holds the microphone and the reins of power.

Questions for Discussion

A. The Challenges for Evangelical Egalitarianism

Under this heading, I list three challenges evangelical egalitarians must face in defending their views.

1. Do you think this list accurately represents the challenges facing evangelical egalitarians?

2. Discuss my assessment of the position of evangelical egalitarians as being questioned from the right about their faithfulness to Scripture and from the left about the consistency of their egalitarianism.

B. The Challenge for Traditionalists

In this section, I express doubt that traditionalists can persuade a contemporary audience by asserting the authority of the New Testament texts that restrict the role of women while ignoring issues of equality and justice as they are posed in modern culture.

1. I think traditionalists could better make their case by learning to view Christian morality not as a list of isolated commands but as a grand vision of the

Christian life in this world. Do you agree? How
might this shift work to the advantage of traditionalists?

2. What changes in women's roles could traditional
   churches make without compromising their commitment to the Scriptures? Or, given the slippery
   slope of these issues, would making such changes
   be an unwise move?

C. The "Benedict Option"

In this section, I summarize the parts of Rod Dreher's
The Benedict Option relevant to this book.

1. Do you agree with Dreher that Christians must be
   prepared to withdraw from the center of American
   (and western) culture to live authentic Christian
   lives?

2. Discuss my contention that *The Benedict Option*
   helps us reframe the issue of women and church
   leadership by questioning the presupposition that
   the church is a social institution like others in
   American society.

D. The Church as a Social Institution

Until the recent past, general American society considered the church to be a valuable social institution. Many
churches were eager to embrace this role and the privileges it entailed. But a large minority of American society no longer views the church positively.

1. Discuss my contention that American churches may soon discover that they sold their soul to the devil by accepting the obligation to contribute to the common good in return for certain social privileges.

2. Discuss my prediction that retaining its social privileges at the price of its Christian identity may soon be the greatest temptation churches face.

E. Experts and Bureaucrats

Contemporary churches have become bureaucracies administered by experts.

1. Has the modern church assimilated a bureaucratic model of institutions? Do you think such assimilation is a problem?

2. Discuss my charge that the recent push to place women in the ministry and administration of churches is in part due the church's prior assimilation of the modern bureaucratic view of institutions and the expert model of the professions.

F. The Professional Ministry

1. Do you agree with my argument that professionalizing the ministry introduces into this activity many alien and sub-Christian motives?

2. Answer and discuss my question, "Would a church without paid, professional clergy *need* to discuss whether to hire a woman minister?"

G. The Theater Stage

In this section, I point out the negative effects of changing the church from a table-centered fellowship to a stage-centered audience.

1. Discuss your ideas about what the church loses and gains in the transition from a table-centered fellowship to a stage-centered audience.

2. Do you think I am correct that the stage-centered focus of modern churches creates unnecessary occasions for envy and possessiveness of the spotlight?

3. Discuss my idea that meeting in houses as extended families would render irrelevant many of the issues stated in the subtitle and discussed in the first three chapters of this book?

H. A Different Order

1. Discuss the feasibility and the advantages and disadvantages of returning to the New Testament (especially in Paul's churches) way of organizing churches?

2. How could the New Testament ideal of the church as an extended family be applied to modern institutional churches in ways that lessened the pressure to assimilate completely modern culture's progressive values?

3. Lastly, discuss the series of questions I asked above: "What if the church were still a family that met around a table to share the Supper, to pray for each other, and listen to the Scriptures read? And what if the church's ministers were those who actually served without pay and its leaders were those whom the people felt compelled to follow because of the authority of their lives? And what if there were no theater, no stage, and no microphone? Would we be discussing the issue of women in leadership? Would churches be divided into egalitarians and complementarians?"

About the Author

Ron Highfield (PhD, Rice University) is Professor of Religion at Pepperdine University, Malibu, California. He is the author of *Great is the Lord: Theology for the Praise of God* (Eerdmans, 2008), *God, Freedom & Human Dignity: Embracing a God-Centered Identity in a Me-Centered Culture* (Intervarsity Press, 2013), *The Faithful Creator: Affirming Creation in an Age of Anxiety* (Intervarsity Press, 2015), and a contributor to *Four Views on Divine Providence* (Zondervan, 2011).

Made in the USA
San Bernardino, CA
16 September 2017